Hello, my name is Clancy.

My name is ______________________________.

I am in Year __________.

My teacher is ______________________________.

Track your progress

As you complete pages in this book, trace over the matching letter here.

b o

l a e

h k t

1 2

w v j

GREAT WORK!

Yeah!

u y

WELL DONE!
Yippee!

1
2
as in "six"

1
2

TOP WORK!
Wow!

Before you begin writing ...

Here are the 3Ps that will help you with your writing: posture, pencil grip and paper position. You will be reminded about these as you work through the book.

Posture

- Relax your arms.
- Sit back in your chair.
- Make sure your back is straight.
- Put your feet flat on the floor.

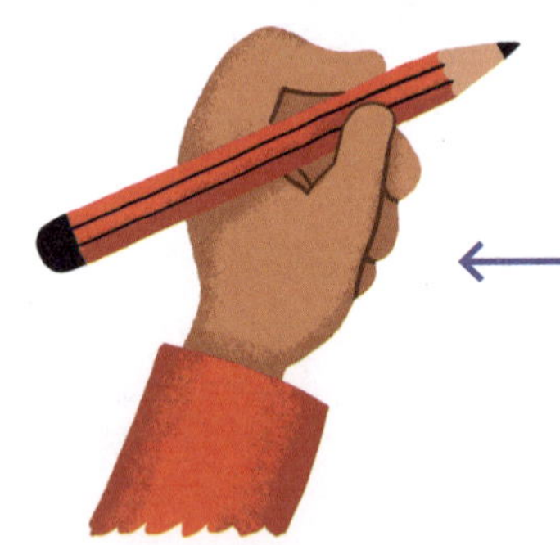

Pencil grip

Hold your pencil like this.
(Not too tightly!)

Left-handed

Right-handed

Paper position

Use your non-writing hand to steady the paper.

Left-handed

Right-handed

Hand and finger warm-ups

Crocodile snaps (whole arms)

Start with one arm straight above the head and the other extended down one side of the body. Snap the hands together, like a crocodile snapping its jaws. Repeat, but reverse the arms.

Open, shut them (hands)

Open, shut them. Open, shut them.
Give a little clap!
Open, shut them. Open, shut them.
Lay them in your lap.
Repeat.

Spider push-ups (fingers)

Place the fingertips together and bend and straighten the fingers while pushing the fingertips against each other.

Letters that do not change

Trace the patterns.

Some letters change so that they can join up.

Some letters do not change.

The letters b, o, g, q, s, c, d and e do not change.

We'll start with these ones.

Have you checked your posture, pencil grip and paper position?

Have you done your warm-ups?

Trace and then copy the letters and words.

above
on
below

b b b b b b b b b

b

big bigger biggest

big

break breaks breaking

break

behind below before

behind

Trace and then copy the letters.

Have you checked your posture, pencil grip and paper position?

Have you done your warm-ups?

octopus

Trace and then copy the letters and words.

above
on
below

o o o o o o o o

o

on off out over

on

open opening opened

open

order orders ordered

order

Trace and then copy the letters.

above
on
below

OXFORD UNIVERSITY PRESS

Have you checked your posture, pencil grip and paper position?

Have you done your warm-ups?

Trace and then copy the letters and words.

above
on
below

g g g g g g g g

g

go goes going gone

gleam gleams gleaming

grace gracious graceful

Trace and then copy the letters.

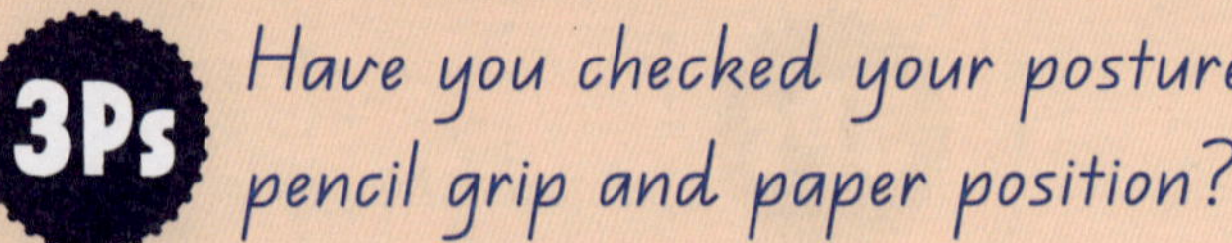

Have you checked your posture, pencil grip and paper position?

Have you done your warm-ups?

Trace and then copy the letters and words.

above
on
below

q q q q q q q q

q

quiet quieter quietest

quiet

quick quicker quickest

quick

quokka quail quoll

quokka

Trace and then copy the letters.

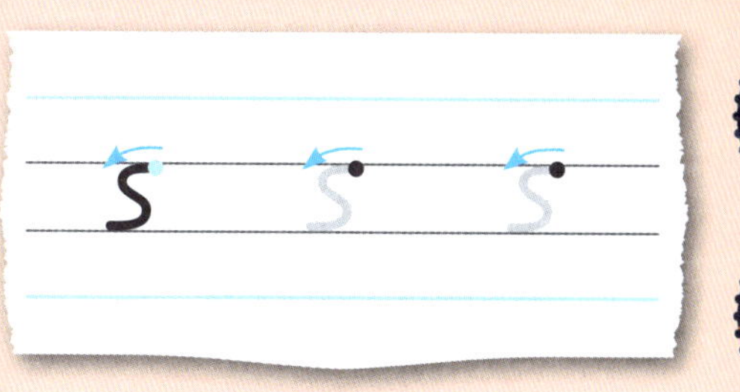

Have you checked your posture, pencil grip and paper position?

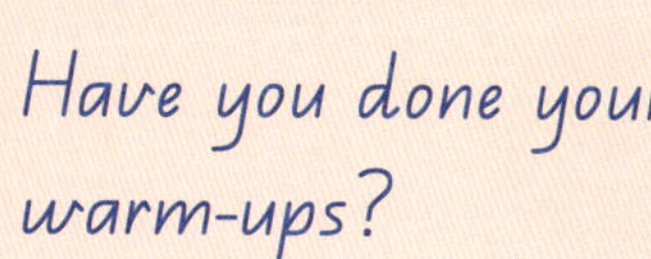

Have you done your warm-ups?

Trace and then copy the letters and words.

above
on
below

s s s s s s s s

s

sleep sleeping slept

sleep

silly sillier silliest

silly

some someone something

some

Trace and then copy the letters.

Trace and then copy the letters and words.

above
on
below

c c c c c c c c

c

can can't could couldn't

can

cook cooking cooked

cook

close closed closing

close

Trace and then copy the letters.

Have you checked your posture, pencil grip and paper position?

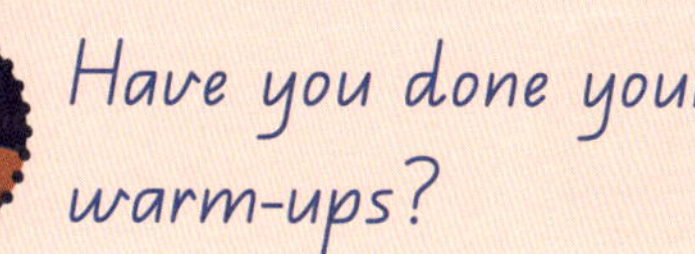

Have you done your warm-ups?

drums

Trace and then copy the letters and words.

above

on

below

d d d d d d d d

d

dry dries drying dried

dry

did did not didn't

did

dislike dislikes disliked

dislike

Trace and then copy the letters.

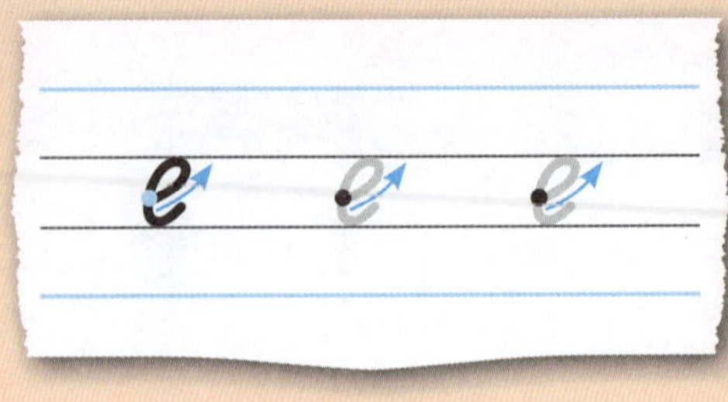

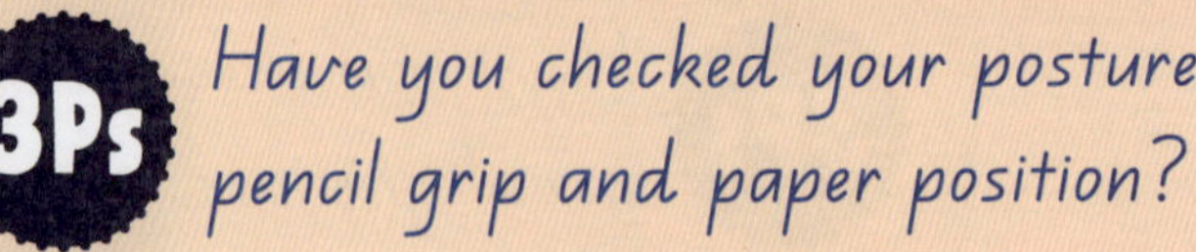

Have you checked your posture, pencil grip and paper position?

Have you done your warm-ups?

echidna

Trace and then copy the letters and words.

above
on
below

e e e e e e e e

eat eats eating eaten

eat

excite exciting excited

excite

eight eighteen eighth

eight

Trace and then copy the letters.

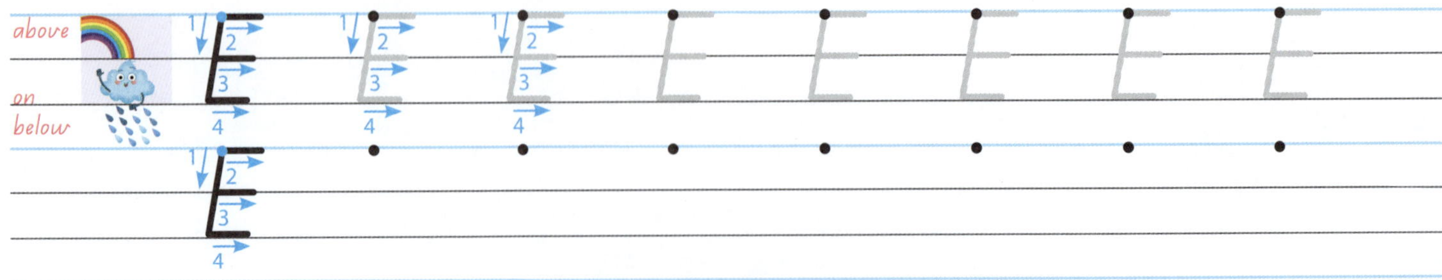

Adding exit flicks

The next group of letters have exit flicks added to them.

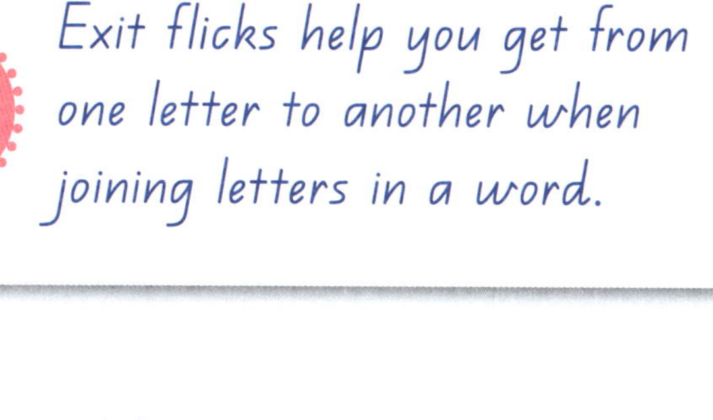

These letters start like this.

Then we add an exit flick.

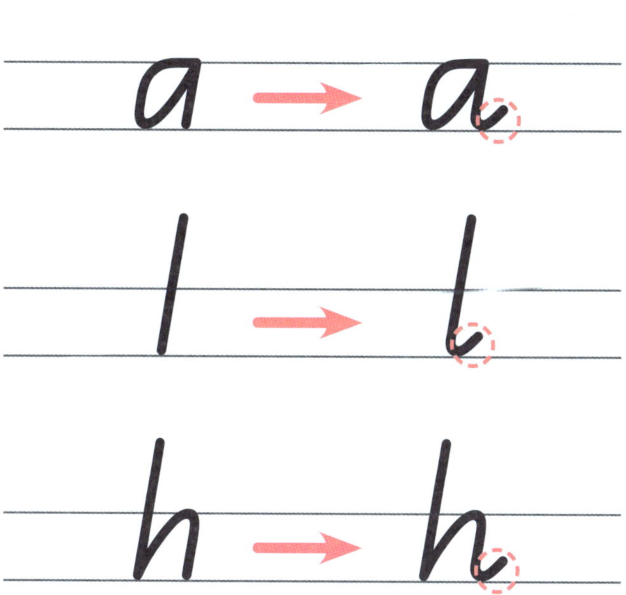

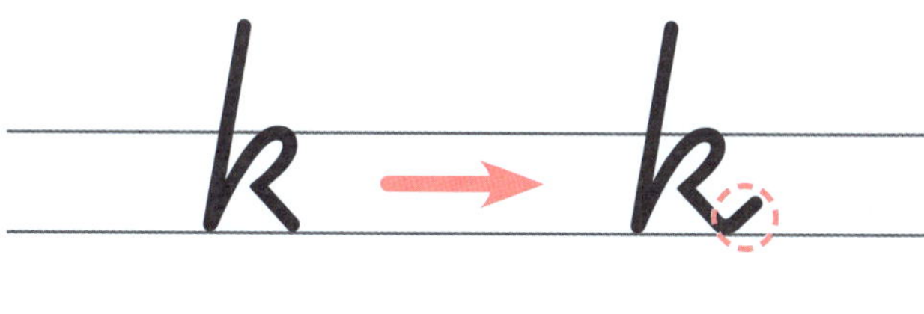

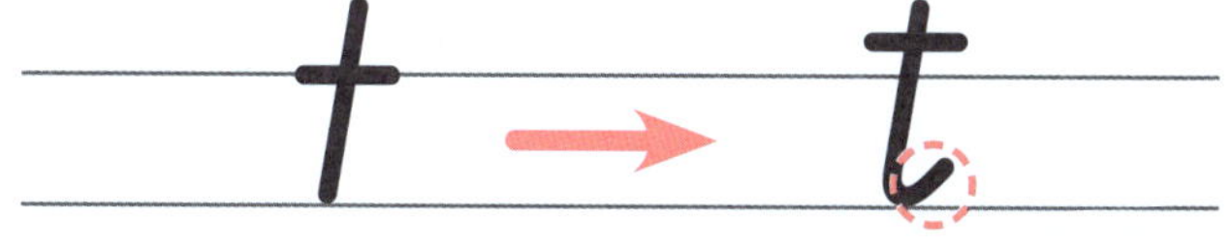

The letter t has two changes. An exit is added, and the crossbar lifts up a bit higher.

a a a

3Ps Have you checked your posture, pencil grip and paper position?

Have you done your warm-ups?

avocado

Trace and then copy the letters and words.

above
on
below

a a a a a a a a

a

as gas ace aces aced

as

add adds added

add

ago age ages aged

ago

Trace and then copy the letters.

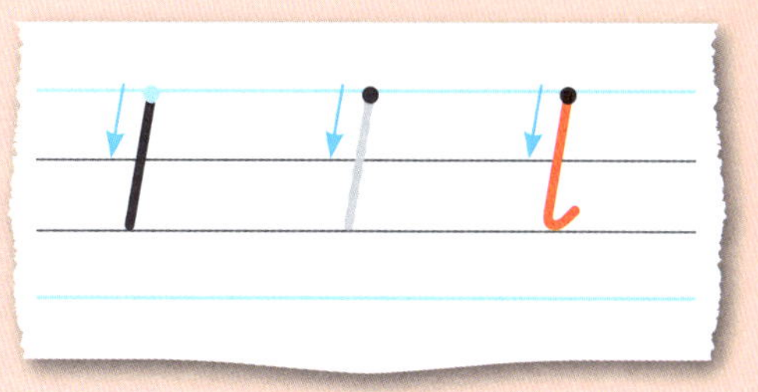

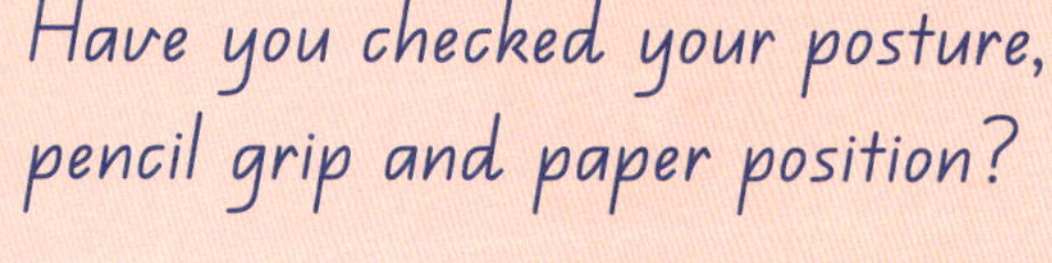

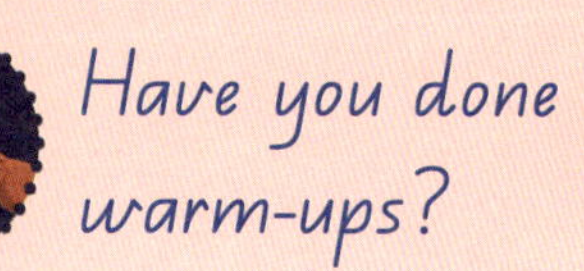

lips

Trace and then copy the letters and words.

above
on
below

l l l l l l l l

log logs logged

log

lad lads leg legs

lad

lag lags lagged

lag

Trace and then copy the letters.

above
on
below

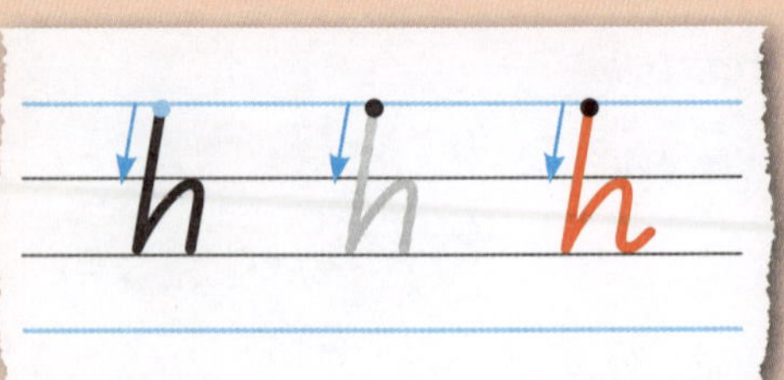

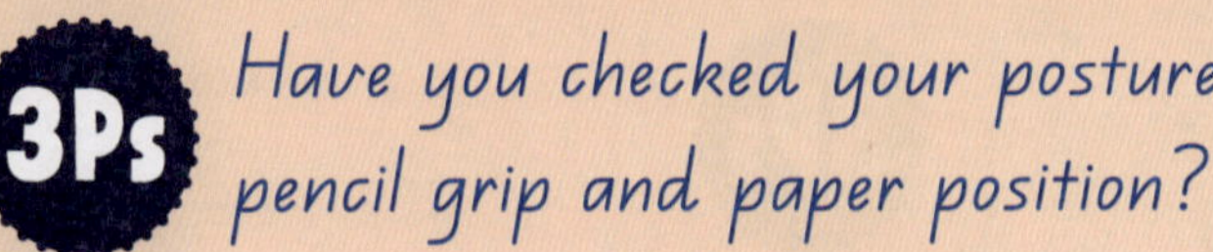

Have you checked your posture, pencil grip and paper position?

Have you done your warm-ups?

helicopter

Trace and then copy the letters and words.

above
on
below

h h h h h h h h

h

hold holds held

hold

hog hogs hedge hedges

hog

hood hoods hose hoses

hood

Trace and then copy the letters.

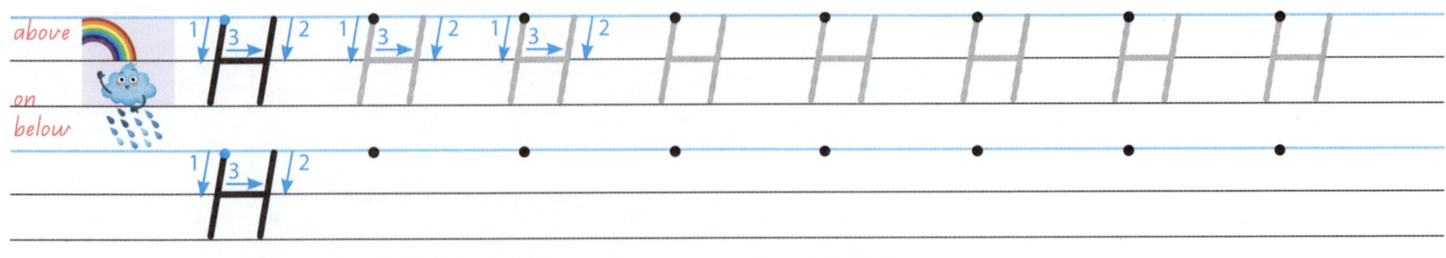

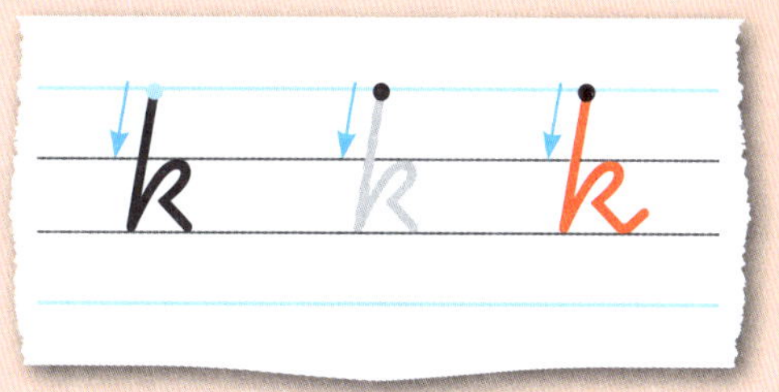

Have you checked your posture, pencil grip and paper position?

Have you done your warm-ups?

key

Trace and then copy the letters and words.

above
on
below

k k k k k k k k

k

koala koalas kebab kebabs

koala

keel keels kale keg kegs

keel

book books beak beaks bake

books

Trace and then copy the letters.

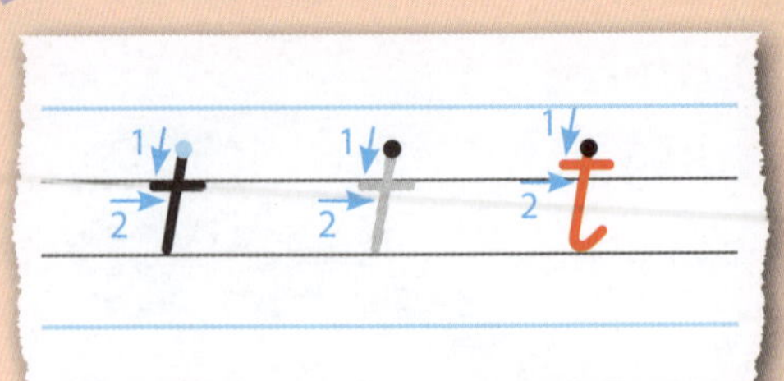

Have you checked your posture, pencil grip and paper position?

Have you done your warm-ups?

Trace and then copy the letters and words.

above
on
below

t t t t t t t t

t

take takes took toll

take

tale tales task tasked

tale

tag tags tall that talk

tag

Trace and then copy the letters.

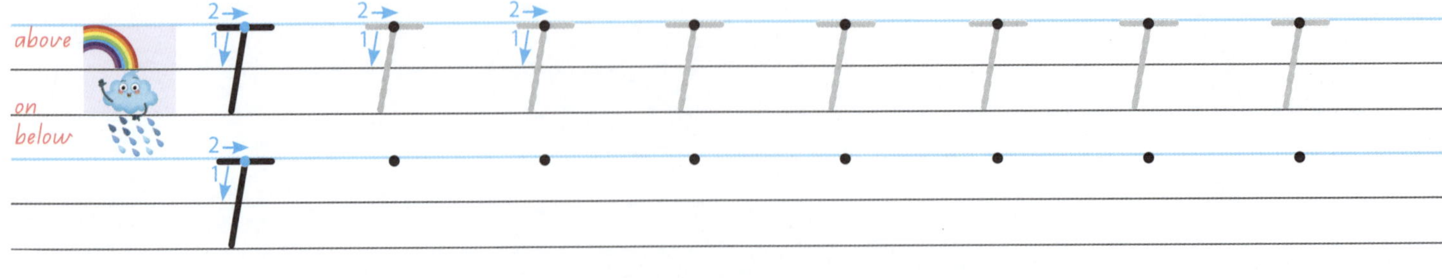

Adding rounded entry flicks

Trace the patterns.

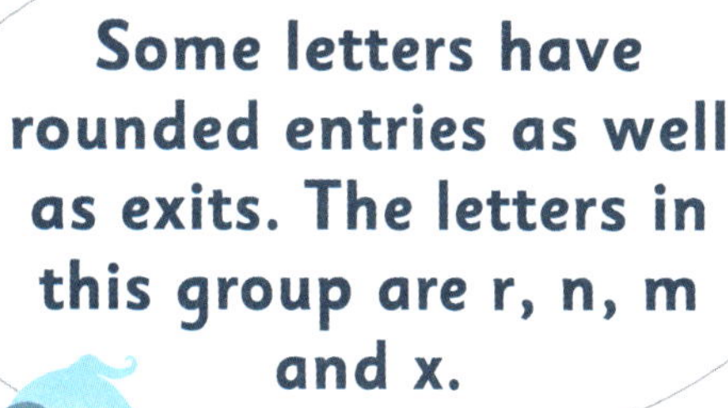

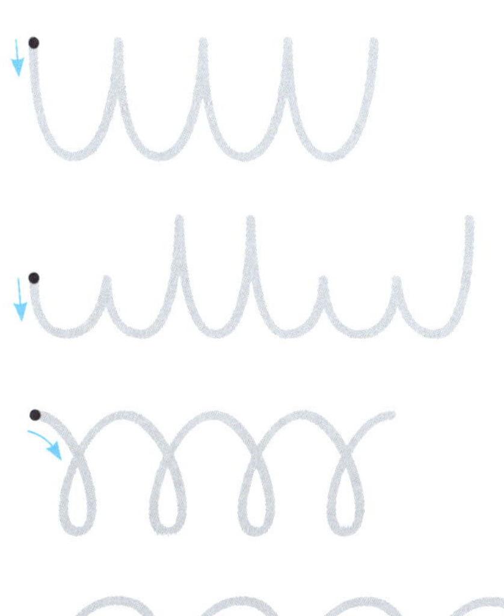

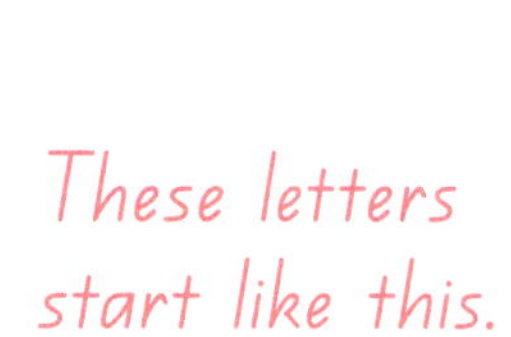

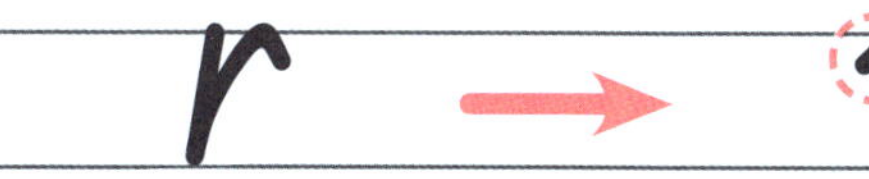

These letters start like this. Then we write them with an entry flick.

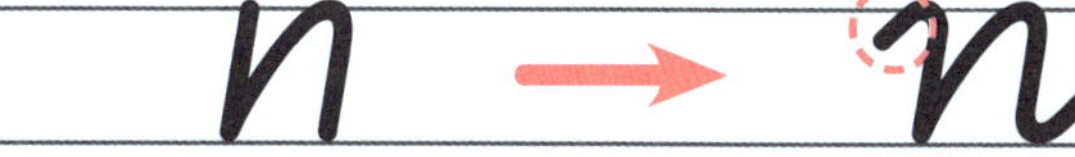

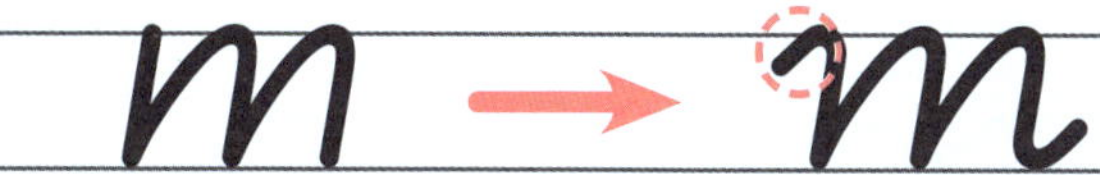

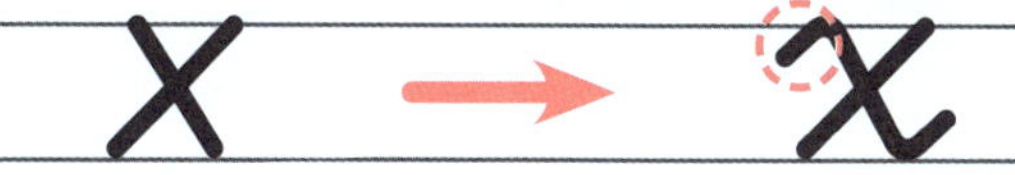

Have you checked your posture, pencil grip and paper position?

Have you done your warm-ups?

Trace and then copy the letters and words.

above
on
below

r r r r r r r r

r

rest roast reach react

rest

real red read reads

real

robot rocket rash rashes

robot

Trace and then copy the letters.

Have you checked your posture, pencil grip and paper position?

Have you done your warm-ups?

Trace and then copy the letters and words.

above
on
below

n n n n n n n n

n

nest nests nose noses

nest

nod nods note notes

nod

need neck note near

need

Trace and then copy the letters.

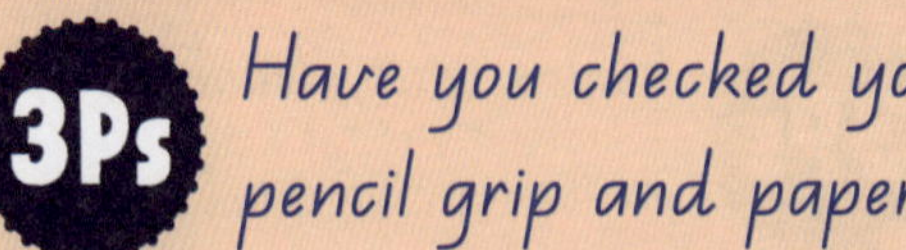

Have you checked your posture, pencil grip and paper position?

Have you done your warm-ups?

mowing

Trace and then copy the letters and words.

above
on
below

m m m m m m m m

m

most mast mask masks

most

make malt mat matted

make

market mash moat moss

market

Trace and then copy the letters.

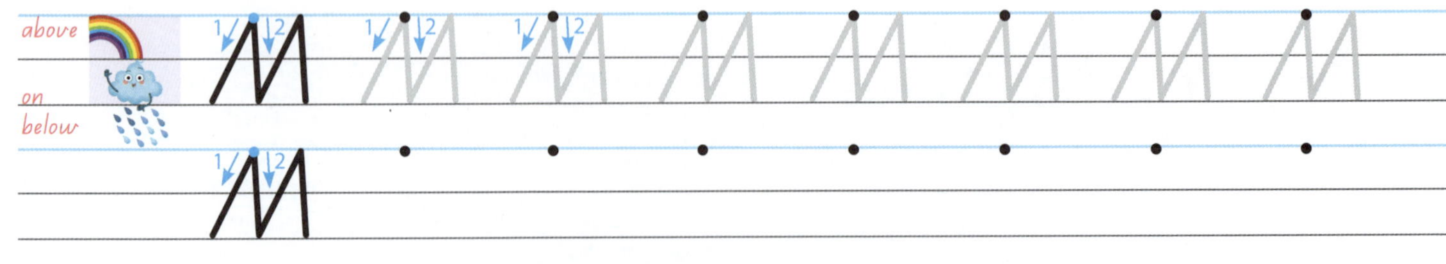

Have you checked your posture, pencil grip and paper position?

Have you done your warm-ups?

x as in "six"

Trace and then copy the letters and words.

above

on

below

box boxer next extreme

box

tax flex lax ox oxen

tax

exact extra exam exams

exact

Trace and then copy the letters.

Adding pointed entry flicks

Trace the patterns.

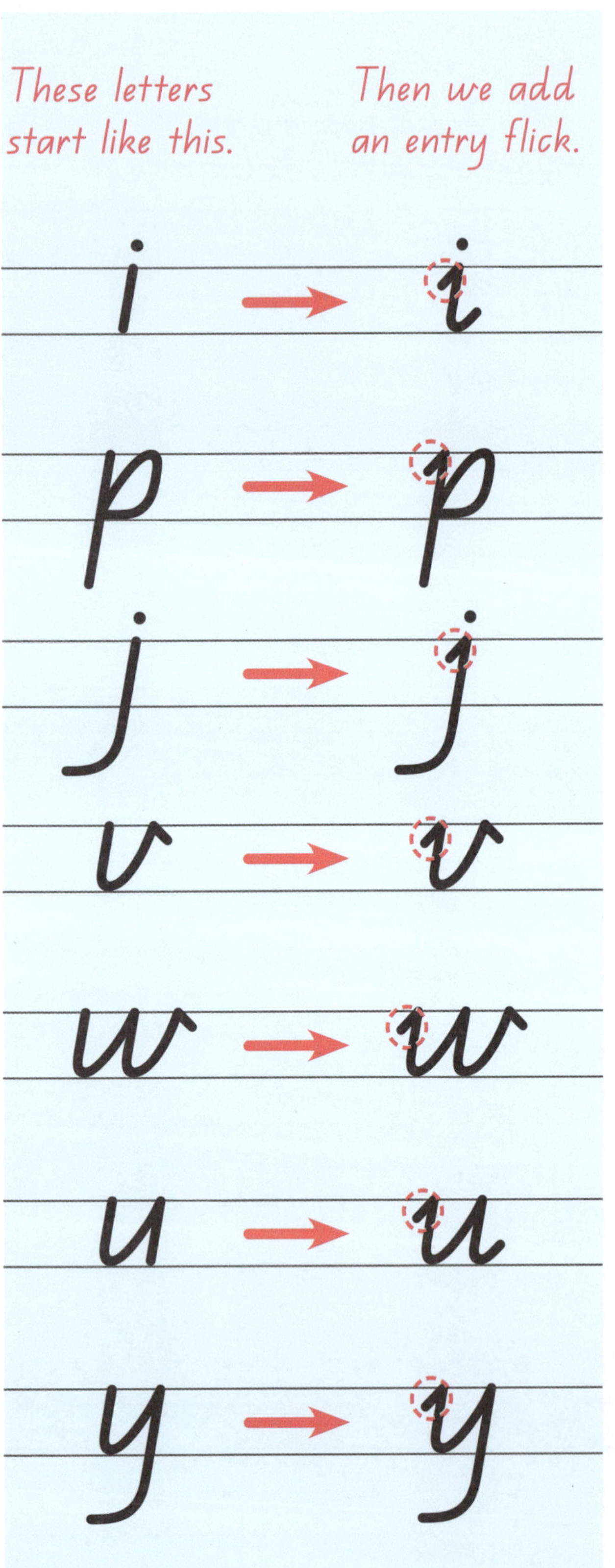

The next group of letters have pointed entries added to them. The letters in this group are i, p, j, v, w, u, y.

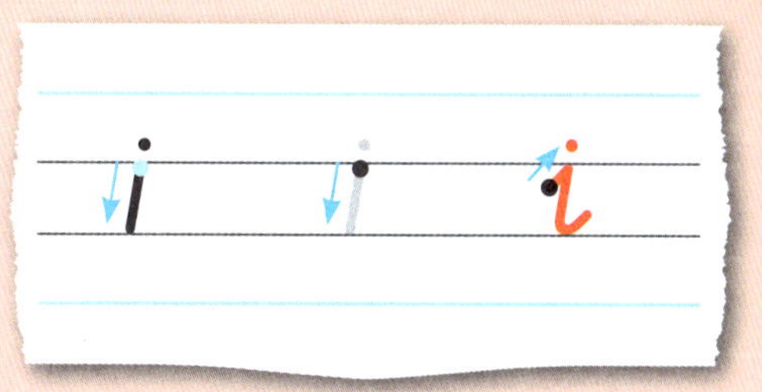

Have you checked your posture, pencil grip and paper position?

Have you done your warm-ups?

Trace and then copy the letters and words.

above
on
below

i i i i i i i i

i

into ink it is isn't inn

into

in inside instead imagine

in

intend interesting insert

intend

Trace and then copy the letters.

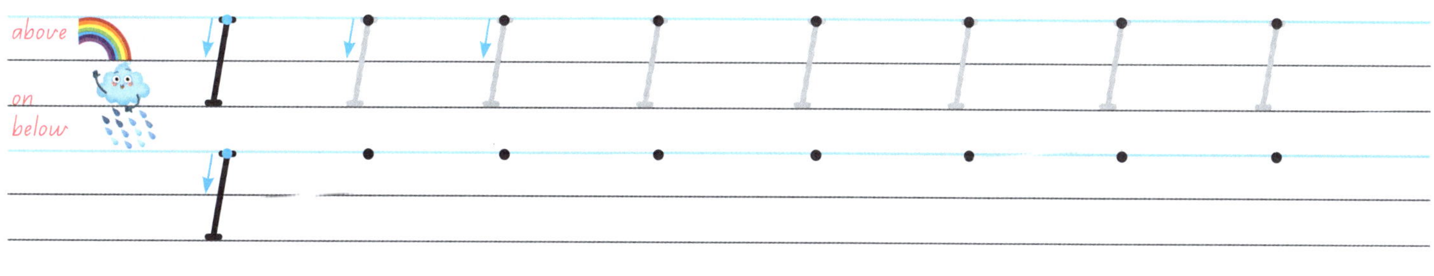

Have you checked your posture, pencil grip and paper position?

Have you done your warm-ups?

Trace and then copy the letters and words.

above
on
below

p p p p p p p p

p

paper patch peach pearl

paper

pancake popcorn pineapple

pancake

peace packet pocket porch

peace

Trace and then copy the letters.

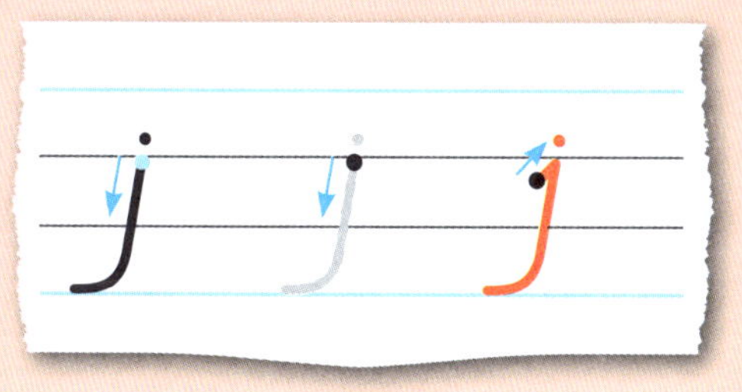

Have you checked your posture, pencil grip and paper position?

Have you done your warm-ups?

Trace and then copy the letters and words.

above
on
below

j j j j j j j j

j

joke jokes joking joked

joke

jog jogs jogging jogged

jog

jacket jellyfish jest jet

jacket

Trace and then copy the letters.

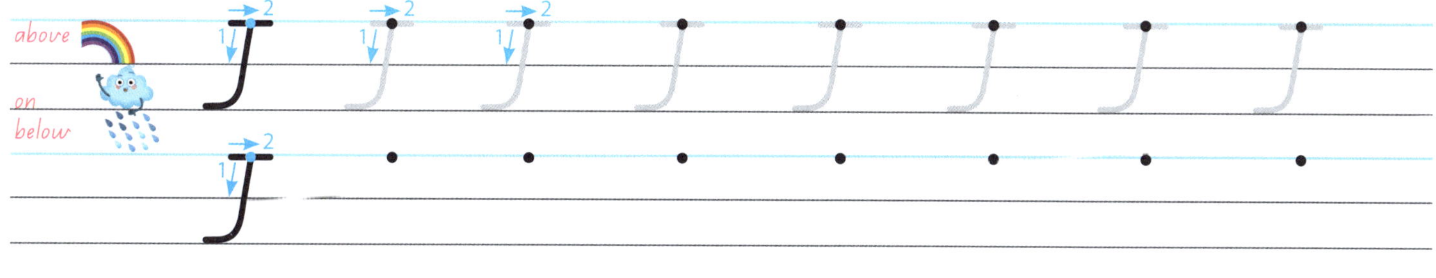

Have you checked your posture, pencil grip and paper position?

Have you done your warm-ups?

Trace and then copy the letters and words.

above
on
below

v v v v v v v v

v

visit visits visitors visited

visit

vast value vain vex vision

vast

voice voices version vent

voice

Trace and then copy the letters.

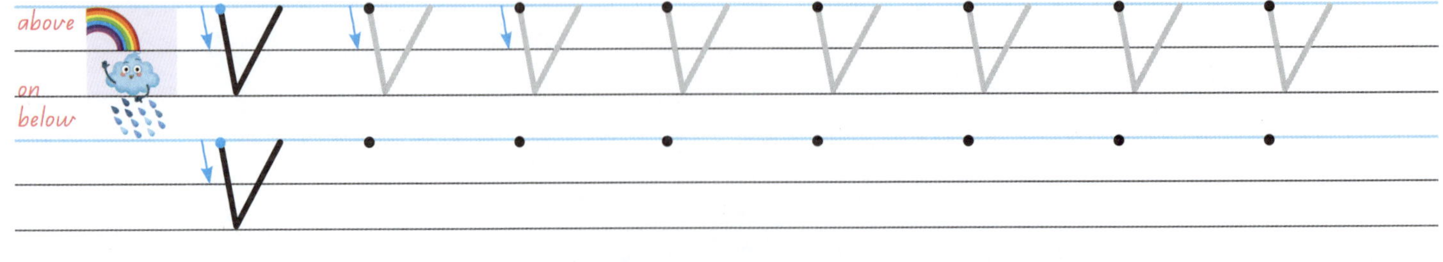

Have you checked your posture, pencil grip and paper position?

Have you done your warm-ups?

Trace and then copy the letters and words.

above
on
below

want wants wanted

walk walking walked

water watering watered

Trace and then copy the letters.

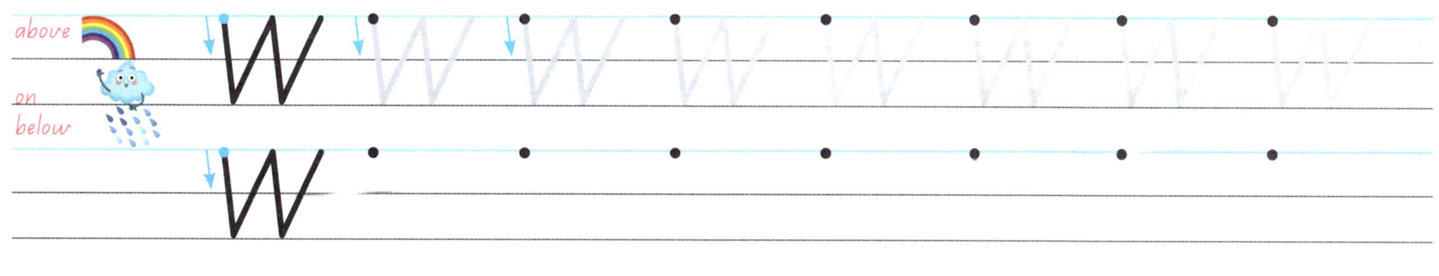

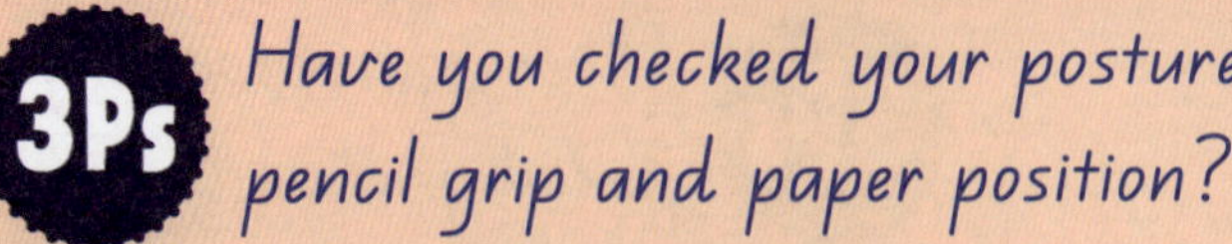

Have you checked your posture, pencil grip and paper position?

Have you done your warm-ups?

Trace and then copy the letters and words.

above
on
below

u u u u u u u u

u

use uses using used

use

undo undone undoing

undo

unpack unpacks unpacked

unpack

Trace and then copy the letters.

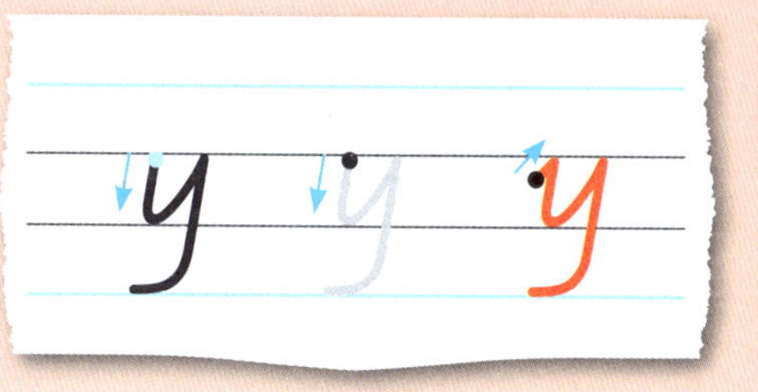

y y y

3Ps Have you checked your posture, pencil grip and paper position?

Have you done your warm-ups?

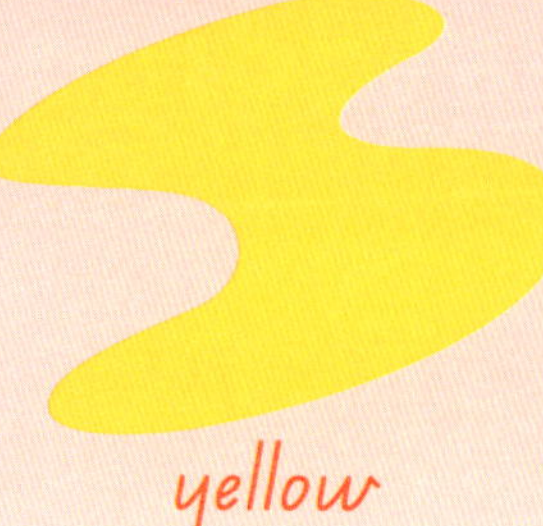

yellow

Trace and then copy the letters and words.

above
on
below

y y y y y y y y

y

you your yours yesterday

young younger youngest

yum yummy yummiest

Trace and then copy the letters.

above
on
below

Y Y Y Y Y Y Y Y

Y

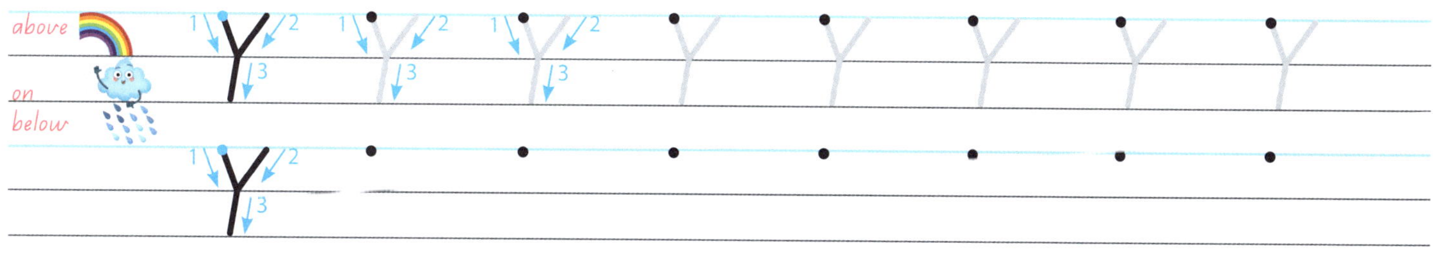

Adding changes to f and z

Trace the patterns.

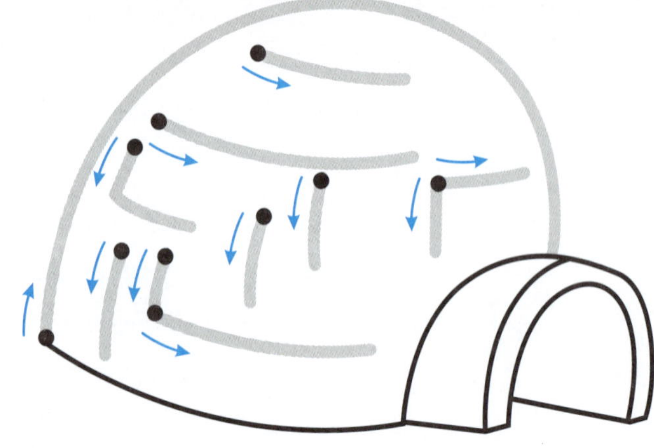

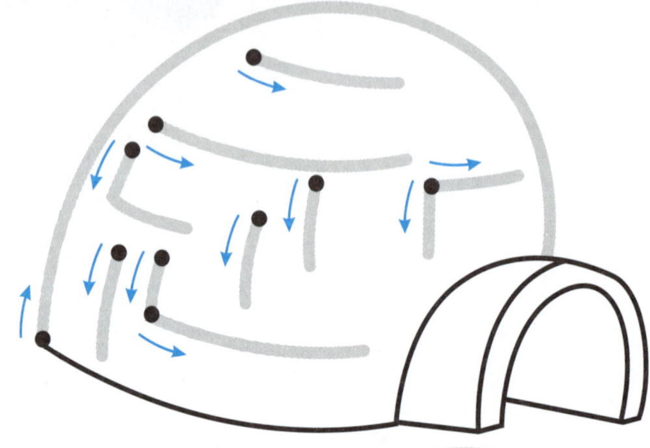

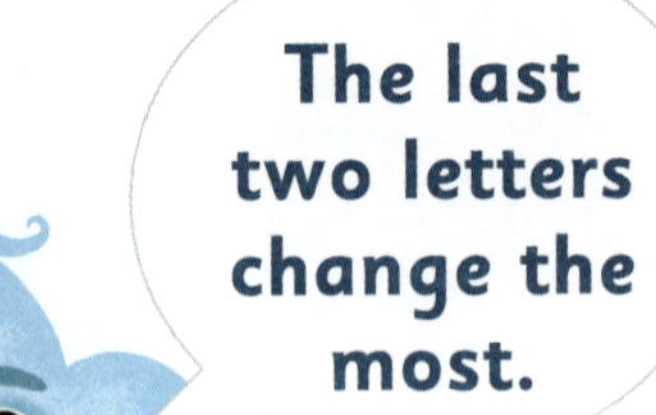

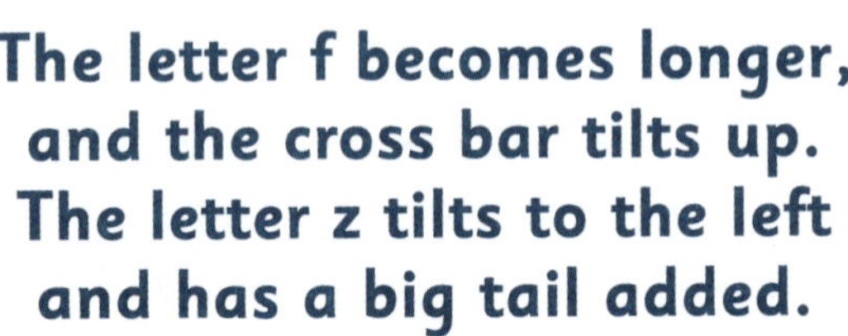

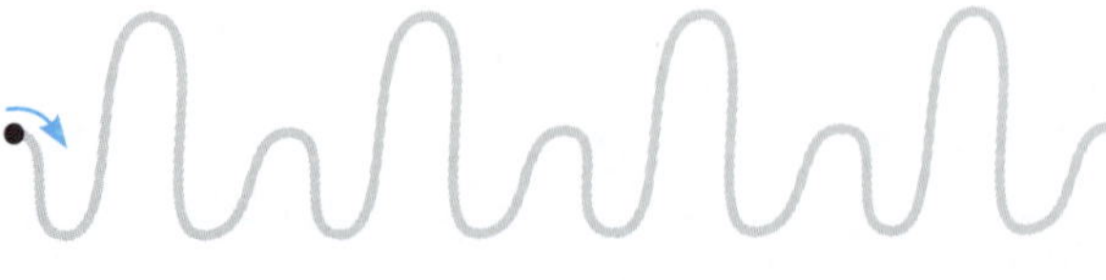

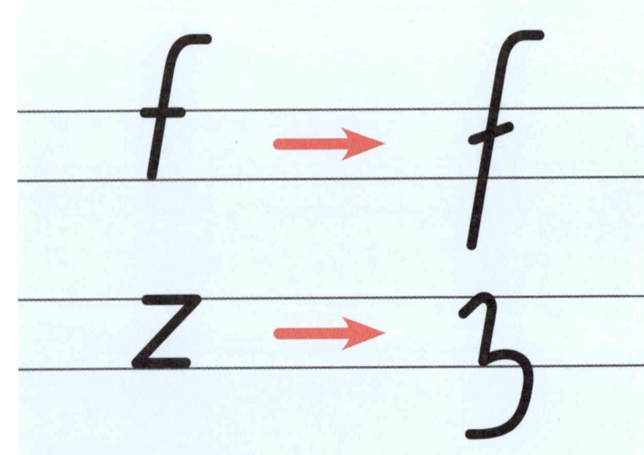

OXFORD UNIVERSITY PRESS

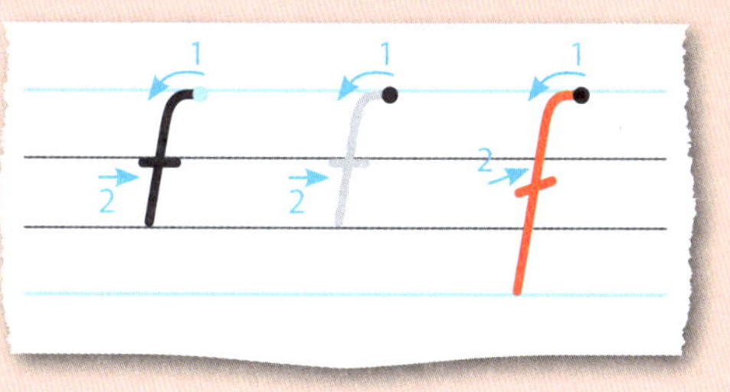

Have you checked your posture, pencil grip and paper position?

Have you done your warm-ups?

Trace and then copy the letters and words.

above
on
below

f f f f f f f f

f

float floats floating

float

fly flying flew

fly

friend friends friendly

friend

Trace and then copy the letters.

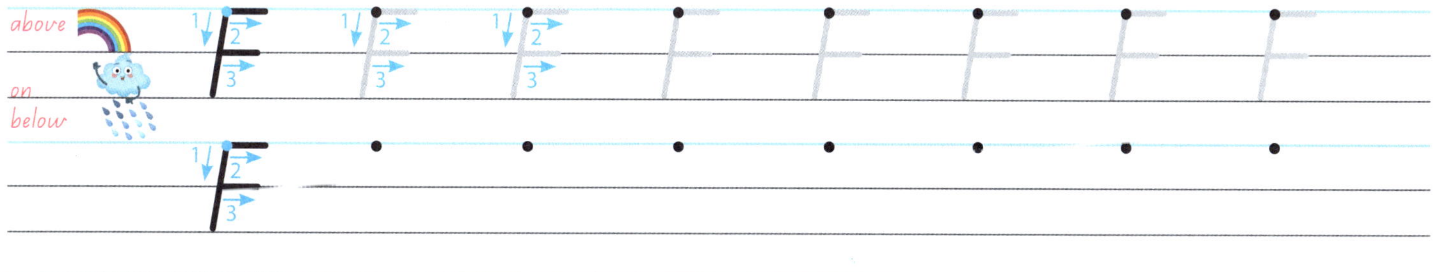

Have you checked your posture, pencil grip and paper position?

Have you done your warm-ups?

zebra

Trace and then copy the letters and words.

above
on
below

zip zipped zipper zigzag

zip

lazy lazier laziest laziness

lazy

puzzle puzzles puzzled

puzzle

Trace and then copy the letters.

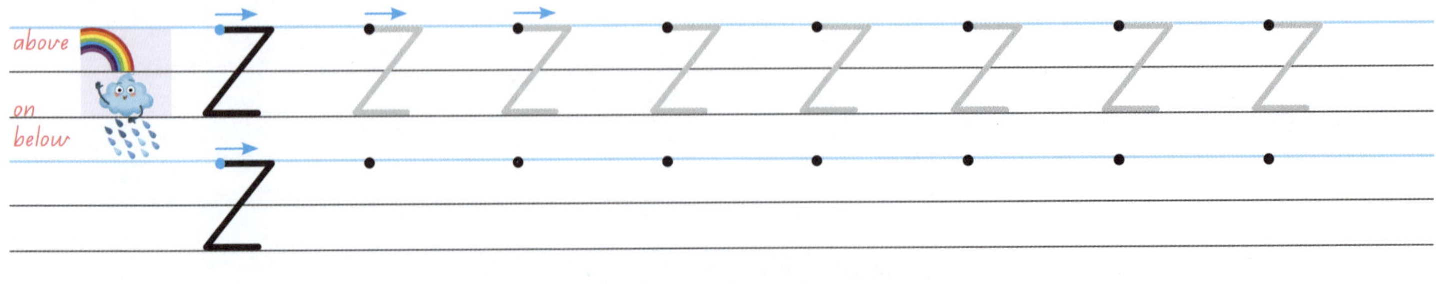

OXFORD UNIVERSITY PRESS

Writing sentences

In this next section, we will practise writing sentences. But first we will do some warm-up patterns.

Trace and then continue each pattern.

Trace and then copy the sentence below.

Ali arrived at the Acropolis

A

at exactly the right time.

a

Choose some interesting words starting with the letter a or A and write them on the lines below.

Self-assessment

Put a circle around your best word on each page. Explain your choice to your teacher or classmate.

Trace and then copy the sentence below.

Benjamin saw a big spider

climbing behind the bench!

Choose some interesting words starting with the letter b or B and write them on the lines below.

Self-assessment

Put a circle around your best word on each page. Explain your choice to your teacher or classmate.

Trace and then copy the sentence below.

Cali cooked a creamy coconut

C

c

Choose some interesting words starting with the letter c or C and write them on the lines below.

Self-assessment

Put a circle around your best word on each page. Explain your choice to your teacher or classmate.

Trace and then copy the sentence below.

Dusty the dog ran in the

puddle and got very muddy.

Choose some interesting words starting with the letter d or D and write them on the lines below.

Self-assessment

Put a circle around your best word on each page. Explain your choice to your teacher or classmate.

Trace and then copy the sentence below.

Eddie came eighth in the egg-

E

and-spoon race on sports day.

a

Choose some interesting words starting with the letter e or E and write them on the lines below.

Self-assessment

Put a circle around your best word on each page. Explain your choice to your teacher or classmate.

Trace and then copy the sentences below.

Faz has fun on his fancy

floaty. Faz's dad watches him.

Choose some interesting words starting with the letter f or F and write them on the lines below.

Self-assessment

Put a circle around your best word on each page. Explain your choice to your teacher or classmate.

Trace and then copy the sentences below.

Gino, get the dog's green lead.

G

We are going to the dog park.

W

Choose some interesting words starting with the letter g or G and write them on the lines below.

Self-assessment

Put a circle around your best word on each page. Explain your choice to your teacher or classmate.

Trace and then copy the sentences below.

Hanya is so happy! Her new

H

house is near a huge beach.

h

Choose some interesting words starting with the letter h or H and write them on the lines below.

Self-assessment

Put a circle around your best word on each page. Explain your choice to your teacher or classmate.

Trace and then copy the sentence below.

I imagined that I invented an

I

incredible dancing robot.

i

Choose some interesting words starting with the letter i or I and write them on the lines below.

Self-assessment

Put a circle around your best word on each page. Explain your choice to your teacher or classmate.

Trace and then copy the sentence below.

Jill wears her jumper in July

but is shaking like a jelly.

Choose some interesting words starting with the letter j or J and write them on the lines below.

Self-assessment

Put a circle around your best word on each page. Explain your choice to your teacher or classmate.

Trace and then copy the sentence below.

Keki saw kangaroos and

K

koalas on Kangaroo Island.

k

Choose some interesting words starting with the letter k or K and write them on the lines below.

Self-assessment Put a circle around your best word on each page. Explain your choice to your teacher or classmate.

Trace and then copy the sentence below.

Lia lives near Uluru with her

family and Lila the lizard.

Choose some interesting words starting with the letter l or L and write them on the lines below.

Self-assessment

Put a circle around your best word on each page. Explain your choice to your teacher or classmate.

Trace and then copy the sentence below.

Max and Mae play melodic

M

music at the school concert.

m

Choose some interesting words starting with the letter m or M and write them on the lines below.

Self-assessment Put a circle around your best word on each page. Explain your choice to your teacher or classmate.

Trace and then copy the sentence below.

Nick and his family wait for

N

the new film to start at nine.

t

Choose some interesting words starting with the letter n or N and write them on the lines below.

Self-assessment

Put a circle around your best word on each page. Explain your choice to your teacher or classmate.

Trace and then copy the sentence below.

Olivia and I open all of our

O

birthday presents at once!

b

Choose some interesting words starting with the letter o or O and write them on the lines below.

Self-assessment Put a circle around your best word on each page. Explain your choice to your teacher or classmate.

Trace and then copy the sentence below.

Choose some interesting words starting with the letter p or P and write them on the lines below.

Self-assessment Put a circle around your best word on each page. Explain your choice to your teacher or classmate.

Trace and then copy the sentence below.

Queenie the quiet quoll creeps

Q

quickly past the quokka.

q

Choose some interesting words starting with the letter q or Q and write them on the lines below.

Self-assessment

Put a circle around your best word on each page. Explain your choice to your teacher or classmate.

Trace and then copy the sentence below.

Rollo saw a bright rainbow

over the tropical rainforest.

Choose some interesting words starting with the letter r or R and write them on the lines below.

Self-assessment Put a circle around your best word on each page. Explain your choice to your teacher or classmate.

Trace and then copy the sentence below.

Sam slept in on Sunday and

S

was late for the soccer game.

w

Choose some interesting words starting with the letter s or S and write them on the lines below.

Self-assessment Put a circle around your best word on each page. Explain your choice to your teacher or classmate.

Trace and then copy the sentence below.

Tam is excited to celebrate

his tenth birthday today!

Choose some interesting words starting with the letter t or T and write them on the lines below.

Self-assessment

Put a circle around your best word on each page. Explain your choice to your teacher or classmate.

Trace and then copy the sentence below.

Uri uses his new crayons to

U

draw a picture for his mum.

d

Choose some interesting words starting with the letter u or U and write them on the lines below.

Self-assessment Put a circle around your best word on each page. Explain your choice to your teacher or classmate.

Trace and then copy the sentence below.

Vicky's family saw vultures flying over the wide valley.

Choose some interesting words starting with the letter v or V and write them on the lines below.

Self-assessment Put a circle around your best word on each page. Explain your choice to your teacher or classmate.

Trace and then copy the sentence below.

Willow would have liked to

W

stay for the whole weekend.

s

Choose some interesting words starting with the letter w or W and write them on the lines below.

Self-assessment Put a circle around your best word on each page. Explain your choice to your teacher or classmate.

Trace and then copy the sentence below.

Mr X, the excited little fox,

explored a complex rabbit hole.

Choose some interesting words with the letter x or X and write them on the lines below.

Self-assessment Put a circle around your best word on each page. Explain your choice to your teacher or classmate.

Trace and then copy the sentence below.

Yesterday, Yindi brought the

Y

yummiest lunch to school.

y

Choose some interesting words starting with the letter y or Y and write them on the lines below.

Self-assessment Put a circle around your best word on each page. Explain your choice to your teacher or classmate.

Trace and then copy the sentence below.

Zahra's popcorn, pizza and puzzle party was amazing!

Choose some interesting words starting with the letter z or Z and write them on the lines below.

Self-assessment

Put a circle around your best word on each page. Explain your choice to your teacher or classmate.

Trace and copy.

a b c d e f g h i j k l m

n o p q r s t u v w x y z

A B C D E F G H I J K L M

N O P Q R S T U V W X Y Z

Trace the numbers.

1 2 3 4 5 6 7 8 9 10

11 12 13 14 15 16 17 18 19 20

Teacher comment